KENT COAST FROM THE AIR

HALSGROVE

PHOTOGRAPHY BY JASON HAWKES

KENT COAST from the Air

First published in Great Britain in 2009

Copyright © Jason Hawkes 2009

All rights reserved. No part of this publication may be reproduced,
stored in a retrieval system, or transmitted in any form or by any
means without the prior permission of the copyright holder.

British Library Cataloguing-in-Publication Data
A CIP record for this title is available from the British Library

ISBN 978 1 84114 780 2

HALSGROVE
Halsgrove House,
Ryelands Industrial Estate,
Bagley Road, Wellington, Somerset TA21 9PZ
Tel: 01823 653777   Fax: 01823 216796
email: sales@halsgrove.com

Part of the Halsgrove group of companies
Information on all Halsgrove titles is available at: www.halsgrove.com

Printed and bound by Grafiche Flaminia, Italy

INTRODUCTION

*K*ent's coastline runs from Broomhill Sands near Dungeness, running north-eastwards along the English Channel before moving directly west and ending at the point where the Darent River enters the Thames at Dartford. For over 178 miles (286km) the coastline passes through some of the most iconic of all of England's coastal scenery, with the White Cliffs of Dover being among the world's most famous landmarks. In this book we begin our journey at Dungeness and end at St Mary's Island on the Medway.

From Dungeness we travel towards Romney Marsh, once a bleak and forbidding region haunted by smugglers, and even today sparsely populated. This wetland area is important for the range and extent of its marshland habitats, boasting an impressive diversity of flora and fauna.

Further on we reach New Romney, the first of the Kent 'Cinque Ports' established in 1155 when, being so close to France, they held strategic military and trading importance. New Romney now lies a good mile from the coast due to the silting of the River Rother. Next comes Hythe, which has also lost its harbour due to silting, a small market town sitting on a broad bay at the edge of Romney Marsh.

Folkestone's fortunes have declined from its heyday as a tourist town which came with the arrival of the railway in the 1840s. Dover is next, famous through its historic associations as a port, and not least for the White Cliffs nearby that epitomize the romantic vision of the British as an Island Race. As the coast swings north, past Deal and on to Pegwell Bay, we come upon the resorts of Ramsgate, Broadstairs, Margate and Herne Bay, which from the Victorian period onwards provided Londoners with their annual escape from the drab toil of city life. Even today these resorts maintain a carefree environment where families can enjoy the traditional pleasures of the seaside.

Our aerial journey nears its end at the Isle of Sheppey and the Medway towns.

The superb aerial photographs in this book provided a fascinating overview of this historic coastline which these days provides the means for thousands to enjoy leisure pursuits including watersports of all kinds, bird-watching, or simply walking the coastal footpaths.

The principal attraction of aerial photographs is that they are literally a bird's-eye view, allowing us to look down on the landscape from a perspective that we never normally see. Such pictures reveal to us things that are normally hidden from view, and often surprise us when we find that what we had imagined the layout of the land to be is in reality quite different. The best practitioners of this genre of photography also strive to capture an aesthetic in the images they take, and these pictures, sometimes quite abstract in appearance, are often strikingly beautiful in their own right.

Jason Hawkes is one of the country's best-known photographers specialising in aerial photography. From his base near London he travels worldwide to produce images for books, advertising and design. Since 1991 he has provided photographs for major international companies including Nike, HSBC, Ford, Rolex, Toyota and BP. The images in this book and the sister publications in the series were specially commissioned by Halsgrove.

For more information regarding Jason Hawkes' work visit www.jasonhawkes.com. For a complete list of titles in this series and other Halsgrove titles visit www.halsgrove.com.

The impressive remains of a redundant technology, the three 'listening ears' at Denge near Dungeness in Kent are the best known of various types of acoustic mirror built along Britain's coast in the early decades of the twentieth century. A forerunner of radar, the sound mirrors were intended to provide early warning of enemy aircraft approaching Britain.

Above: Beach huts on Greatstone beach, Greatstone-on-Sea.

Right: The genteel resort of Littlestone lies on the coast between Greatstone and St Marys Bay at the end of the Dymchurch Wall, the sea defences built by the Romans. Littlestone's name is derived from the shingle on the beach here being smaller than that at Greatstone and Dungeness to the west. The 120ft high red brick watertower was built in 1890 to provide water for the resort.

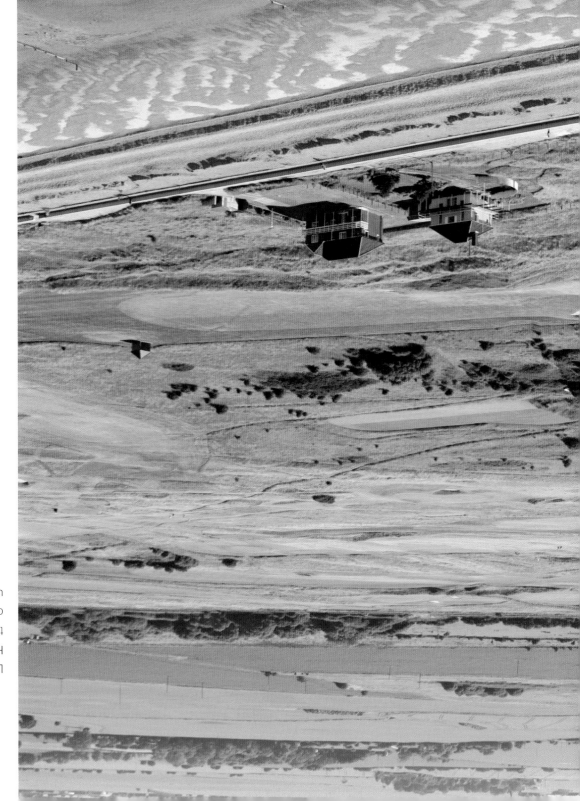

Looking inland over Romney Bay House hotel and the coast road, to the west of Littlestone, with the outskirts of New Romney visible upper left.

Left: The little seaside community of St Mary's Bay lies between Littlestone and Dymchurch. It grew up in the early twentieth century and for a time was known as Jesson.

Above: Breakwater at St Mary's Bay. The coast here is under severe threat from erosion by the sea.

Above: Seaside amusement park at Dymchurch, with the restored Martello Tower (No.24) just visible on the right.

Right: Looking down on to High Street, Dymchurch. Along with the amusement park and the superb beach, the town is famed for the Romney, Hythe & Dymchurch Railway.

Previous page: The Martello Tower (No.25) at Dymchurch.

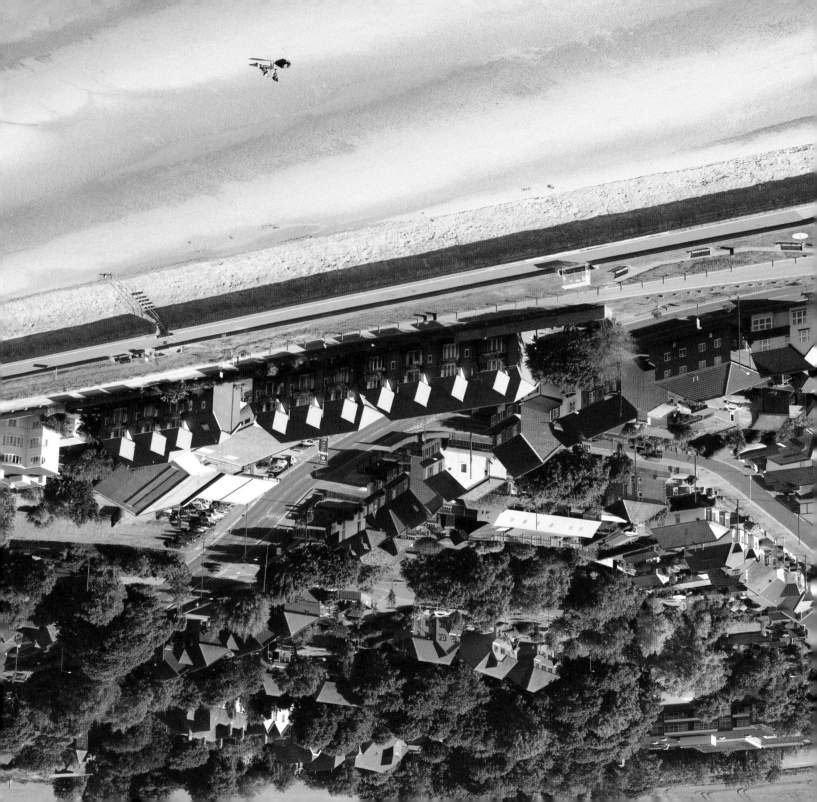

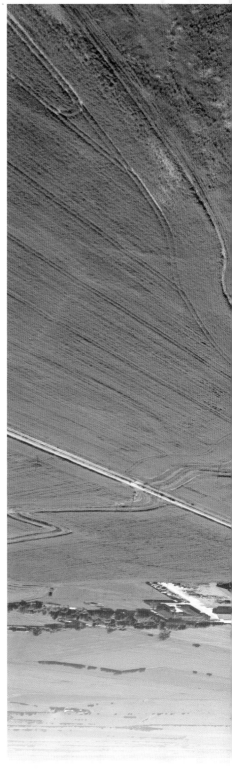

Left and above: Two views over Dymchurch looking down the coast towards St Mary's Bay. The straight course of the Romney, Hythe & Dymchurch Railway can be seen running parallel with the coast.

Above: A superb view up the coast from Dymchurch looking towards Hythe, Sandgate and Folkestone.

Right: Caravans stand in neat rows at a holiday centre between Dymchurch and Hythe. The flat nature of this coastal landscape is clearly shown in the photograph, looking almost due west.

Above: Dymchurch Redoubt was built between 1806–1809 as a supply depot for the chain of Martello Towers that punctuate this coastline. The Redoubt underwent significant re-fortification during the Second World War with bunkers and pillboxes added to its parapets.

Right: This Martello Tower (no.14) stands within the Danger Zone at the eastern edge of the Hythe Ranges and at one time was used to display the red flag to show that firing was in progress. The ranges are still used for live firing by the military and were originally part of the Royal School Of Musketry situated on Barrack Hill in Hythe.

Above: Looking down on Marine Parade, Hythe.

Left: Boats drawn up on the shore at Hythe. Although declining, fishing is still an important trade on this coast.

A bird's-eye view over the corner of Stade Street and South Road, with the cricket ground top right. Hythe, one of the Cinque Ports, sits on the 'Garden Coast' four miles west of Folkestone and 16 miles south-west of Dover.

A wide promenade overlooks a long stretch of beach, and behind the seafront the town is sited on level ground with most of the immediate area being residential. A five-minute stroll along Stade Street brings you to the Royal Military canal, built during Napoleonic times as a defensive measure.

Left: Pretty verandahs on seafront properties at Hythe.

Above: The Royal Military Canal separates the beach-side links course from quiet residential streets, Hythe.

Previous page: Sandgate esplanade.

Above: A superb panoramic view over Sandgate.

Right: Looking inland over Sandgate with the Metropole, once a hotel and now largely apartments, dominating the clifftop.

Previous page: The view east over Folkestone, with Dover in the far distance.

Left: The opposite view, with Folkstone pier and harbour in the centre ground.

Above and right: Travelling east from Folkstone the distinctive chalk cliffs begin to rise above the coastline. The village of Caple-le-Ferne nestles on the clifftop.

Following page: Lorries bound for the Continent line the A20 on their way down to the harbour at Dover. In the foreground is Samphire Hoe Country Park.

Left and above: The historic importance of Dover harbour lay in its proximity to France, being at the narrowest part of the English Channel. It remains a major ferry port and ferries crossing between here and the Continent have to negotiate their way through a constant stream of shipping crossing their path.

Right: The view looking out to sea over the port of Dover with Dover Castle dominating the high ground to the right.

Following page: Dover Castle has the longest recorded history of any major castle in Britain, its origins dating back to the Iron Age. Soon after the Battle of Hastings, in the autumn of 1066, William the Conqueror spent eight days at Dover strengthening fortifications which had only recently been rebuilt by the defeated Harold. The great square tower, or keep, was built in the 1180s for King Henry II. St Mary's Church stands on the seaward side of the castle, and next to it is the Pharos lighthouse, built by the Romans.

Above and right: The Port of Dover offers a comprehensive range of services for freight drivers and operators who use it as a gateway to and from Continental Europe.

All aboard! Freight traffic at Dover.

Left and above: Around three sailings per hour leave the freight terminal at Dover bound for Continental ports.

Above: The southern breakwater, Dover harbour.

Right: Langdon Hole cliffs lie just east of Dover harbour. The Saxon Shore Way footpath and the White Cliffs Country Trail provide walkers with exhilarating views.

Above and right: The White Cliffs, while more stable than many that bound England's coastline, are also victim to erosion. Here, between Fan Point and South Foreland, the effects of such erosion can clearly be seen.

South Foreland lighthouse remains a striking landmark on the White Cliffs of Dover. This elegant historic building was the first to have an electrically powered signal and was used in experiments by Faraday and Marconi. Today, visitors can climb to the top of the lighthouse and enjoy views across east Kent and the English Channel.

Right and below: The coastal footpath leads around the edge of the grounds which houses a disused lighthouse and St Margaret's Bay windmill – a smock mill built in 1928 and originally used to aid drainage.

Left and above: The war memorial at St Mary's Bay honours those who served with the Dover Patrol, the naval force guarding this coast against attack and invasion in the Great War. The monument was erected in the early 1920s.

Above: The White Cliffs Country Trail advances along the cliff's edge between St Margaret's Bay and Kingsdown.

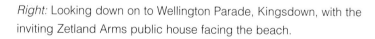

Right: Looking down on to Wellington Parade, Kingsdown, with the inviting Zetland Arms public house facing the beach.

Above: Summer holiday weather at the beach huts, Kingsdown.

Right: Originally built during the reign of Henry VIII as part of a chain of coastal artillery defences, Walmer Castle has evolved over time into an elegant residence.

Walmer Castle became the official residence of the Lord Warden of the Cinque Ports in 1708. The Duke of Wellington held the post of Lord Warden for 23 years. Now in the care of English Heritage, the beautiful gardens surrounding the house include a commemorative lawn, woodland walk, croquet lawn and a working kitchen garden. The castle is one of the region's major tourist attractions.

Dinghies await the weekend at Walmer.

Above: The flotsam and jetsam of working fishing boats at Walmer.

Right: Deal Castle is one of the finest Tudor artillery castles in England. It is among the earliest of a chain of coastal forts, which also includes Calshot, Camber, Walmer and Pendennis Castles. It was built by order of King Henry VIII and guarded the sheltered anchorage of 'the Downs' - the stretch of water between the shore and the hazardous Goodwin Sands, a graveyard of ships.

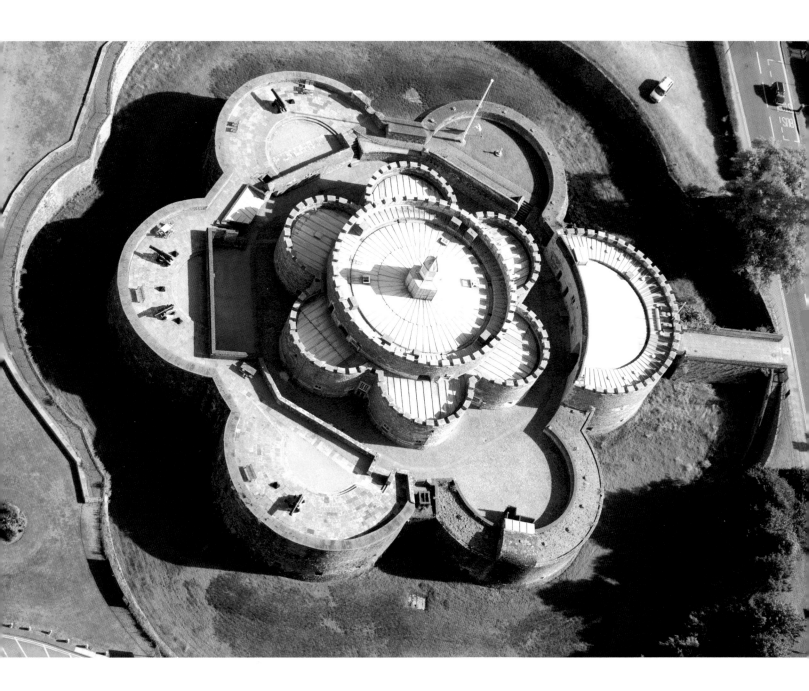

73

A magnificent view looking almost due south over Deal, with the pier visible mid distance.

Following page: The northerly run of the coast beyond Deal is followed by the Saxon Shore Way footpath and Princes Drive, the road that serves the sparse settlements along this stretch of shore. This view also shows the Sandwich Flats in the far distance, the mud and sand banks that lie along the coast, and the towers of the disused power station at Richborough.

Previous page: The Rover Stour runs out past Richborough to the coast at Shell Ness.

Above: Pegwell Bay looking inland towards St Lawrence and Newington, on the outskirts of Ramsgate, seen right.

Right: Ramsgate harbour provides ferry crossings to Dunkirk and Ostend.

Ramsgate began life as a fishing village but its proximity to the Continent brought about the construction of Ramsgate Harbour, begun in 1749 and completed about 1850. The harbour has the unique distinction of being the only Royal Harbour in the United Kingdom. While fishing continues, much of the harbour is now given over to leisure boating, with an 800 berth marina. This in turn supports the trade in tourism.

While it is the harbour that defines Ramsgate, its wide sandy beaches have appealed to holidaymakers from Victorian times onwards.

Previous page: Looking over East Cliff into the outskirts of Ramsgate.

Above and right: The harbour and town of Broadstairs, and (right) further along the coast towards North Foreland.

Above: The bandstand, Broadstairs.

Right: Tidal bathing pool, Broadstairs.

Left and above: The tide's out and it's time to play on the sands at Viking Bay, Broadstairs.

Exclusive and genteel clifftop properties alongside Cliff Promenade, Broadstairs.

Looking south over Broadstairs – the very name exudes quiet gentility as captured in this superb aerial photograph.

Left and above: The lighthouse at North Foreland. A lighthouse first stood here in 1499, but the present tower was built and added to in the years between 1793 and 1890. North Foreland was the last Trinity House lighthouse to be automated.

Above: Kingsgate Castle stands on the cliffs above Kingsgate Bay, Broadstairs. It was built for Lord Holland in the 1760s and has now been converted into apartments.

Right: This ruined tower now guards a tee on the North Foreland golf course.

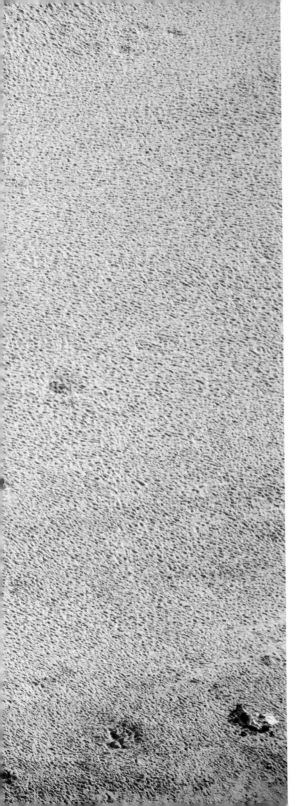

While the English passion for taking holidays at home has yet to return to the heyday of yesteryear, there are still plenty of reasons for visiting traditional seaside resorts. On a sunny days the sands and tidal swimming pool alongside the Eastern Esplanade at Cliftonville, close by Margate, match almost anything to be found abroad.

The encircling arm of the pier wall at Margate, at low tide.

Above and left: Sunshine and shadows on the harbour jetty, Margate.

Above and right: Seaside delights at Margate, with the Royal Terrace (right) exemplifying the elegance of a bygone era.

Above and right: Next door to Margate, Westgate-on-Sea boasts
two sandy beaches that have remained a popular tourist attraction
since the town's development in the 1860s

Above Westgate Pavilion and theatre is built within what was originally a bandstand at Ledge Point.

Right: A fine view over Westgate Bay.

Following page: A superb panorama looking inland over the Isle of Thanet, with Westgate-on-Sea in the foreground.

Left: View inland over Westgate-on-Sea, with Epple Bay on the right.

Above: Birchington.

Another wonderful shot looking into the heart of the Isle of Thanet with Birchington foreground.

Beach huts line the shore along
The Parade west of Birchington.

Reculver guarded the north end of the Wantsum Channel that separated the Isle of Thanet from the rest of Kent. The Romans had originally built a fort here in AD43, when the sea was almost a mile away. By the early nineteenth century the sea had encroached so far that the villagers moved inland.

Above: The two twelfth-century towers of the ruined church stand among the remains of the Roman fort and a Saxon monastery. Reculver Country Park offers superb walks and a visitor centre.

Right: Herne Bay takes its name from the village that stands a mile or so inland. The sheltering sweep of the sea defense is known as 'Neptune's Arm'.

Above: A striking image of the lonely pier head at Herne Bay. This once was connected to the landward end of the pier but storms in the late 1970s destroyed much of the central parts, and in 1980 the damaged portion was removed leaving the end section isolated.

Right: The view inland over Herne Bay.

Above and left: Known as the 'Pearl of Kent', Whitstable is famous for its oysters, which have been collected in the area since at least Roman times. Whitstable's distinctive character and ambience is popular with tourists, and its maritime heritage is celebrated with the annual Oyster Festival in July.

Above: Looking across the Isle of Sheppey at Leysdown-on-Sea.   *Right:* Caravans lined up at Leysdown-on-Sea.

Left: Signs of severe coastal erosion at Warden, Isle of Sheppey.   *Above:* Looking south-east along the coast towards Minster.

Above: From Sheerness towards Halfway Houses, Isle of Sheppey.   *Right:* The view near Queensborough at the mouth of the River Medway.

Above: The area at the mouth of the River Medway contains some of the most important salt marsh habitat in Britain. Every winter, thousands of avocets, dunlins, teal and wigeons flock to the Medway – swimming in the waters, feeding on the mudflats, and flying in the skies overhead.

Right: This is also an important seaway with complex tides and shallows offering real challenges to sailors. Here we look from an oil jetty at Kingsnorth power station on the Hoo Peninsula towards mainland Kent and the Isle of Sheppey.

Left: Hoo Fort was built in the 1860s on an island covering the inner navigable channel of the River Medway. In the Second World War, the fort was used as an observation post.

Above: The view south over Gillingham Reach on the River Medway towards Gillingham, with Chatham beyond.

St Mary's Island was originally a series of marshy inlets, but was enclosed and developed during the great expansion of the dockyard in the late nineteenth century. This expansion involved the building of the three huge dock basins which separate St Mary's Island from the 'mainland'.